Through the Seasons with
SNOOPY

Based on the Charles M. Schulz Characters
Designed by Terry Flanagan

Happy House Books

Copyright © 1983 by United Feature Syndicate, Inc. Produced in association with Charles M. Schulz Creative Associates. All rights
reserved under International and Pan-American Copyright Conventions. Published in the United States by Random House, Inc.,
New York, and simultaneously in Canada by Random House of Canada Limited, Toronto. Library of Congress Catalog Card
Number: 82-60892 ISBN: 0-394-85627-9
Manufactured in the United States of America 1 2 3 4 5 6 7 8 9 0

January

On New Year's Day Snoopy made a resolution.
His future is clear! He has found the solution!
With a little more practice he knows he'll go far
And be billed by the Ice Capades as their top star!

"Snoopy looks like a fool, if you ask my advice,"
Lucy says to herself as she glides on the ice.
"That stupid beagle thinks he's so great!
What makes him think he knows how to skate?"

February

No one asked Charlie Brown, "Will you be mine?"
Not one kid has sent him a valentine.
Not one dopey card from one dopey kid.
He wishes he knew what it was that he did!

Charm, decides Snoopy, just cannot be taught.
It cannot be borrowed. It cannot be bought.
There are those who just have it—for instance, me.
And then there's Charlie Brown....

March

On St. Patrick's Day there's quite a scene
With everybody wearing green,
And Linus has his heart set on
Meeting a little leprechaun!

Patty has changed her name to Colleen
And says Charlie Brown should be Charlie Green!
Snoopy's decided that it might be better
To spend the day as an Irish setter.

April

Sally is sporting a new Easter bonnet,
And Woodstock is building a nest upon it.
Lucy made eggs that she painted and dyed
And knows exactly where to hide.

Flowers are blooming, the sky is sunny.
It's a perfect day for the Easter bunny,
And the Easter beagle is spreading joy
To (almost) every girl and boy!

May

On Memorial Day Lucy sells lemonade,
And Peppermint Patty is in the parade.
The trumpets sound as bands march by.
Balloons are dancing in the sky.

Charlie Brown rides past in an open car,
But who is the day's outstanding star?
That shining example of style and grace—
World War I's first flying ace!

June

Charlie Brown laughed and said, "Good grief!
The last day of school! What a relief!"
Linus, of course, was the first in his class,
And Peppermint Patty was happy to pass.

Hurrah for summer! Hurrah for vacation!
But Snoopy has no time for relaxation.
He believes while others may have their fun,
A beagle's work is never done!

July

On the Fourth of July there's so much to do—
Like swimming and having a barbecue!
Sally's hoping that Linus thinks she looks cute
In her red-white-and-blue-striped bathing suit!

As evening falls across the sky
Exploding colors rise on high!
Snoopy thinks a fireworks display
Is the best way to say "Independence Day!"

August

It's too hot for playing baseball or tennis.
Lucy declared that the heat was a menace.
Charlie Brown said, "Let's go someplace to swim!"
"It's too hot to move," said Lucy to him.

On National Dog Day it was Snoopy's ambition
To be given, at least, some recognition—
The Nobel Prize? A ribbon? A bone?
The fate of a genius—alas, he's alone!

September

"Labor Day signals the end of summer.
We must march to the beat of a different drummer,"
Charlie says with a shrug. Linus adds, "That's the reason
They say that each thing has its very own season!"

"A season," says Sally, "for buying new shoes,
For crayons and pencils and notebooks to choose,
And a fancy new blouse and a skirt I can wear...
And a hat for my head, and a bow for my hair."

October

Although Lucy calls him Blockhead and Bumpkin,
Linus waits patiently for the Great Pumpkin.
He's sure that his pumpkin field is sincere
And that the Great Pumpkin is bound to appear.

Goblins and ghosts wander down the street,
Stopping to ask for a Halloween treat.
Who follows behind them, draped in white?
It's the ghost of a beagle on Halloween night.

November

A leg for Linus, a wing for Lucy,
White meat for Sally that's tasty and juicy.
As he gets his plate there is no need to check—
Charlie Brown knows he'll be stuck with the neck.

Snoopy is thankful, as well he might be,
And Woodstock is thankful, while perched in his tree.
On Thanksgiving Day the thought makes him perky
That no one mistakes him for being a turkey!

December

Snoopy is ready to lead the way
For Santa's reindeer and Santa's sleigh.
He knows he'll look nifty, he knows he'll look regal.
He'll call himself Snoopy the Red-Nosed Beagle!

While around a little Christmas tree
Voices sing an ancient melody...
"Good will to men and peace on Earth..."
To celebrate a baby's birth.